Splash!

Robert Kaufman

Contents

Rigby®

A Harcourt Achieve Imprint

www.Rigby.com
1-800-531-5015

Mountain View Elementary

Water Works

Hello, I'm Dewey the Water Drop. Water is very important. Have you ever thought about all the ways we use water?

Water goes into many foods we make.

Water helps make some of the electricity we use.

We also use water to have fun!

Water on Earth

This is a picture of Earth taken from space. Water in oceans, lakes, and rivers covers about 71 percent of Earth's surface.

71%
Water

29%
Land

Wow! So how does all that water move around?

The Water Cycle

1. The sun warms the oceans. Some heated water turns to vapor and rises into the air.

2. The vapor cools in the air and becomes clouds.

3. Water falls from the clouds as rain.

4. Rainwater goes into rivers that renew the ocean.

Salt Water

Most of Earth's water is salt water found in the oceans. Oceans are salty because rivers flowing into the ocean bring salt from rocks and soil with them.

Atlantic Ocean

Pacific Ocean

N

Fresh Water

People and most animals use fresh water. Fresh water comes from lakes, rivers, and even underground. A very small amount of Earth's water is fresh water.

Many U.S. cities get their water from the Great Lakes.

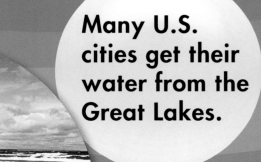

Rivers provide drinking water to people and animals.

Pumps pull drinking water out of the ground.

Glaciers are nature's frozen rivers.

Most fresh water is frozen or too far away to use.

Water and Animals

Animals need water to survive. Animals use water in rivers, lakes, and streams for drinking or finding food.

Everybody loves a cool drink.

Animals like whales and dolphins spend their whole lives in water.

Water and People

People need water for many reasons. Water is very important for our health. Water also helps us grow food. We must make sure we always have enough water.

Your body has over four gallons of water in it!

Plants that we eat must have water to grow.

We can use very little of Earth's water. We need to protect and renew our supply.

Saving Water

I'll show you how to use water wisely. Let's take a tour of a home. It might be a lot like your home. Come on!

Dishes can go in the dishwasher without being rinsed. Run a dishwasher only when it is full.

Turn off the sink faucet while you scrub the dishes.

Side Dish

You can save enough water to fill a fish tank every day by running a dishwasher only when it's full.

The bathroom is a great place to save water. Here's how!

Take a short shower instead of a bath. Showers use much less water. Time yourself to see how fast you can get clean!

Turn off the water while you soap up or put shampoo in your hair.

Turn off the water while you brush your teeth.

ANTICAVITY TOOTHPASTE   NET WT. 6.2 OZ (175g)

EXTRA WHITENING

Showers at Sea

Because fresh water is so rare on a ship, people onboard have to turn off the water while they soap up!

We can save water outside the house, too!

Find out what the weather will be like. If it is going to rain, remind adults to turn off sprinklers.

5-Day Weather Forecast

Monday	Tuesday	Wednesday	Thursday	Friday
Sunny	Sunny	Cloudy	Rainy	Rainy
High: 80°	High: 79°	High: 77°	High: 71°	High: 70°
Low: 59°	Low: 55°	Low: 57°	Low: 53°	Low: 54°

Do not use a garden hose to wash a car. Instead, use a bucket filled with water.

Be a Water Saver

You learned how water is found in many places. You also learned how we use water. But the most important thing you learned is how to save water.

Now you know all about water and how to save it!

Here's a checklist you can use to save water in your home.

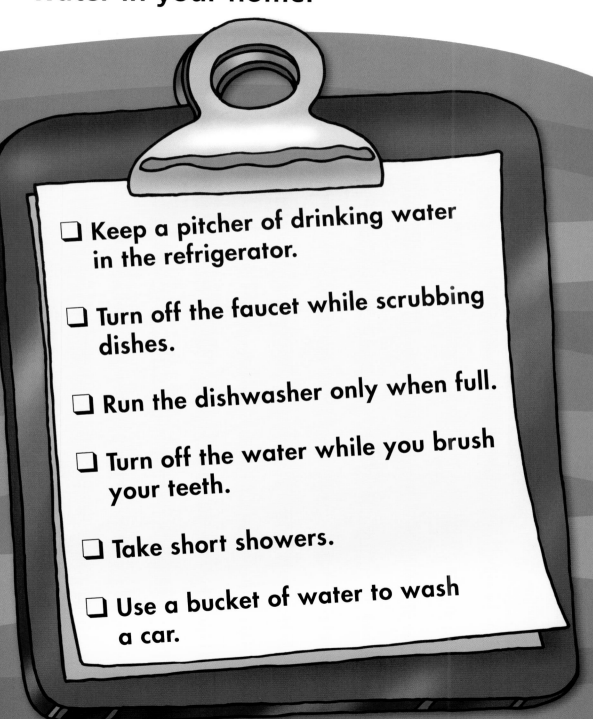

- ❏ Keep a pitcher of drinking water in the refrigerator.

- ❏ Turn off the faucet while scrubbing dishes.

- ❏ Run the dishwasher only when full.

- ❏ Turn off the water while you brush your teeth.

- ❏ Take short showers.

- ❏ Use a bucket of water to wash a car.

Index